PRIVATE PITCH

PRIVATE PITCH

Poetry by Karen Butier Basiulis

PRIVATE PITCH
© 2024 Karen Basiulis
ISBN: 979-8-218-44868-4

First Edition, 2024

Printed in the United States of America

Edited by Cynthia Murray
Cover Design by Ryan A Woods and Karen Basiulis
Layout Design by Cal Sabatini

*To
the memory of
my Croatian grandparents,
the two I knew, and the two I only heard about,
who left a legacy of
immigrant courage, peasant hands,
hard work, and apple pie.*

Hvala Puno.

CONTENTS

PREFACE

This book is the culmination of many years of writing poems on notepads, napkins, envelopes, sheet music, and newspapers. Some of my poems still start out that way. **PRIVATE PITCH** is a collection that spans over 40 years of taking those scribbles to poetry classes and workshops and shaping them into actual poems. I wrote a couple of poems in this book when I was in college, some at various seminars and workshops through the years, and many since retiring in 2014.

In music, perfect pitch is the ability to name exactly what note is being sung or played. We who were not given this gift must soldier on despite our imperfection and keep up. The poetry in **PRIVATE PITCH** explores family, food, and tradition and how they serve to both expose and inform the masks we wear to hide our imperfections, our pain, our fears—our private pitch—from the world. By dropping a few of those masks in this book, I have discovered that what we protect so fiercely is often not as frightening as the masks we wear to cover it..

May this book do the same for you.

PRELUDE

The past is never dead. It's not even past.

–William Faulkner

SUMMER FRUIT

It's late afternoon in my old yellow kitchen
in my little yellow bouncy chair, and I am
giggling and bouncing, giggling and bouncing
as my mother stands at the stove.
The old farm table holds pride of place in the kitchen,
the wall covered in wallpaper showing faded
herbs and flowers rising above it what seems like
a hundred feet.
Parsley, sage, rosemary, and thyme—
a future pop song on that greasy wall in our rickety house
on the wrong side of the tracks.

My grandfather walks by on the way to his room,
hanging his cane on the hook above my head.
Kako si, draga moja malena? he says to me in Croatian.
How are you, my dear little one?
His overcoat, long and dark, hangs from his bent body
like a curtain that is too big
for the window it's supposed to dress.
His sturdy oak cane, curved in his withered hand,
with its strong rubber tip on the end, makes a dull thud
as he plods deliberately and slowly through
the winter of his life.

My father follows him into the kitchen
and puts a galvanized bucket of fruit on the table,
an invitation to my mother
to turn it into pie or cobbler or jam.
I don't remember what fruit it was, but it wasn't apples.
Apples were the family business;
they were picked in the fall.
This was summer, so it could have been some
plump and blushing apricots or juicy peaches
or Santa Rosa plums or sweet little cherries
from the stone fruit trees at the ranch that were there
just for us.

That sturdy old farm table now holds pride of place
in my kitchen and my grandfather's cane
sits in my umbrella rack,
its curve and rubber tip exactly as they were
that day long ago.
I live in the city now, but still anxiously await the first
apricots and peaches and cherries of summer,
standing over the sink gorging as their juices
run down my chin.

Apricot in hand, I feel the farm table watching me
like a doting aunt,
and I turn slowly to see them all there—
parents, grandparents, aunts, uncles, cousins—
around that table, eating, talking, laughing,
moving easily from English to Croatian and back again.
The scents of rosemary and lamb, roast potatoes,
fried krostule pastry sprinkled with powdered sugar,
slivovitz plum brandy, and apple pie fill the kitchen,
the promise of a family feast.
Glasses clink to the cries of "Zivio!" and I close my eyes,
breathe deep and slow, absorb the memories.

My eyes still closed, the laughter at the table fades and
I know it is empty once again. My father comes to me now,
salt and pepper hair, khaki pants,
galvanized bucket in one hand,
the other reaching for mine,
and we walk. I am small and safe, and we walk,
through the orchard, past the apples for sale—
the acres of Red Delicious and Golden Delicious,
Newtown Pippins and Bellflowers—
past the long white barn holding the old tractors and tillers,
past the big makeshift BBQ that saw many a
Fourth of July cookout.
We walk to the trees at orchard's end, perched at the foot
of the golden oak-covered hill, the trees that are there
just for us.

And we gorge.

FULL CRATE, 50 CENTS

Summer vacations
my brother and I, up
before dawn to put on the uniform:
old jeans, grungy work shirt
plastic bucket
tied with a rope around the waist.
No time for corn flakes or cartoons.
Sunrise illuminates the berry field maze
and row after row unfolds before me.
I grab an old wooden crate off the truck,
push back the leaves,
pluck the prized ripe olallieberries.
They land in my bucket with a plop.
I trudge down the row,
dragging the crate along like a shackle,
emptying the bucket into it when it's full.

Transistor radios blare,
the sun beats down until my face is berry brown and
melting like the fruit in my half-full crate.
Berry blood stains my clothes, my hair, my face.
With some luck—and a lot of bleach—
it will fade from my thorn-pricked fingers
by the time school starts.

Full crate, 50 cents. Good
experience, says my mother,
who admonishes me to pick faster,
like Johnny and Jackie and Jose who are
somehow better little citizens than I
because they manage an impressive
four crates a day.
Time.
Character.
Self-worth.
Measured in buckets of berries.

No use complaining.
You're old enough to walk,
you're old enough to work.
Child labor laws don't apply, and
in these parts,
Cesar Chavez is the enemy.
Eyes closed to sleep,
the vines hang in front of me still,
and I long for Saturdays,
my brother and me,
corn flakes and chocolate milk,
Bugs Bunny and the Road Runner,
because in those early hours
while my parents sleep,
we're just kids.

THE ZEN OF JAM

Summer.
Bare feet on the lawn,
sun on my face,
body surfing in the ocean,
tanning deep and dark by the pool,
or just lying around with a good paperback mystery.

Only a few precious days of
that for us. When we weren't picking
the fruit that went into these concoctions,
I watched my mother, the farmer's wife,
turn out batches of jams and jellies, pickles and relishes
with names like piccalilli and chowchow,
to be entered in the county fair.
Her sturdy peasant hands—
the legacy passed from her mother
to her and from her down to me—
frantically mashed and stirred,
the steam from pots full of macerated fruit
and Mason jars being boiled and sanitized
filling the kitchen like a sauna,
fogging up my glasses as I walked through—
quickly—since anything that didn't move
was fair game to be mashed and mounded
into one of those jars.

My mother thrived on these maceration marathons,
dreaming of blue ribbons, trophies,
her fifteen minutes of fame.
She got them, dozens of ribbons, best in class,
sweepstakes awards,
steamy fruit frenzies proving fruitful for her ego
and our pantry.

I hated it.
It was hot, humid, hard work.
Summer was supposed to be

bare feet in the grass,
sun on my face, jumping in a pool.
Lazy.

Destiny, karma, call it what you will.
Years later my husband and I bought a house
with a huge fig tree in the yard that bore more fruit than
even my mother could put up.
Squirrels, raccoons, birds feasted, leaving the
sticky, slimy, slippery remains on the patio tile.
When I decided my own sturdy peasant hands had
wiped up their last sticky, slimy half-eaten fig,
I knew my time had come.
Figs, sugar, lemon juice.
I measured, macerated, mashed,
stirred, steamed, boiled,
made friends with Mason jars. I ladled,
checked headspace,
wiped rims, twisted lids just fingertip tight,
gently lowered full jars of jam into
huge pots of steamy water,
boiled them for exactly ten minutes,
slowly lifted them out again and waited,
reveling triumphantly in the little pops
that mean the vacuum seal took hold, that mean
success.

The beach takes a backseat to summer now.
Mason jars line up happily in my kitchen
to receive all things jam—
apricot, berry, peach, cherry, fig.
Though my hands hold the genetic memory
of frantic summer fruit frenzies,
truckloads of county fair deliveries,
I aspire to no ribbons or trophies or sweepstakes,
no exotic concoctions created solely for contests,
but simply to know the satisfying, mesmerizing,
slow stirring, lid popping, bread slathering,
Zen of jam.

CHRISTMAS EVE 1963

It was raining gift wrap.
You almost needed galoshes to slog through it.
Paper and ribbons littered every surface
of the living room—
the floor, the coffee table, the couch—
the gifts they revealed strewn all over,
buried among
all   that   paper:

the doll for me,
the toy fire truck for my brother,
the pajamas for both of us from my grandmother,
and the envelope full of cash from my father to my mother.
The fireplace was burning logs
the tree burning lights
the table burning candles
the night burning down.
Midnight mass beckoned, my mother
asked me to clean up
all   that   paper.

I flew through the room
gathering piles of paper ribbon, gift tags,
the detritus of Christmas,
threw them into the fire.
I didn't stop to watch them burn.
I turned around, smiling with pride at being
such a good girl
and helping, waiting for high praise from my parents.
But they looked at me, foreheads furrowed,
eyes narrowed.
Where is the envelope with the money?

I looked back and forth between the
fireplace and the now immaculate living room.
My father sighed.
It's gone. Up in smoke.
My mother cried.
As if we had money to burn.
I froze.
I was six.

BABA BAKING BREAD

That's what I remember most: the smell of bread baking
in her house, an aroma divinely inspired
to bring joy, to evoke a genetic memory
of comfort,
              safety,
                          home.
My grandfather died when I was a baby, so
she wore the widow's black,
the blouse tucked into a billowy skirt like the one she wore
years before on a boat out of her native Croatia
with two of her little brothers
tucked beneath its folds because
there was only money for one fare.
Black support hose flowed into plain black oxfords
with black laces and a small, sturdy block heel.
She was petite, dainty, curled into herself,
a marked contrast to her middle daughter,
my bold, brash, abrasive mother.

But those hands. Those thick, stocky, peasant hands
would grab and lift and pinch and toss that dough,
the heels of her palms
pushing it, flipping it, punching it
until it begged for forgiveness,
pleaded for a minute to itself.
Only then would she relent,
finally letting it rest and rise,
only to punch it down again
before finally sliding it into the oven,
its scent filling her kitchen and her grandchildren
with home.

Her English was poor,
so we didn't talk much.
But that bread,
warm from the oven,
slathered in butter and jam,
sighed love in any language.

She died when I was very young,
taking the chance for more memories
with her, so it must be enough to remember
that dainty woman dressed in black,
those thick, sturdy peasant hands
pushing
          flipping
                    punching
that dough, that divine aroma, that perfect loaf.
It must be enough to remember
Baba baking bread.

8TH GRADE MATH

Friday nights at 8, lying on my stomach on the floor,
chin in hands, the Brady Bunch
grid unfolding on TV like a human Tic-tac-toe board.
Suburban utopia, pretty and perfect, so unlike my world
I wondered if they had room
for one more kid and how I could apply.

But 8:30 held my breath,
my life in its hands waiting for that invitation to
C'mon Get Happy, waiting for mama bird
to toddle across the screen and kick off her shell,
waiting for my world to be rocked,
waiting for Him.

David Cassidy Keith Partridge, Nirvana.
That smile, those eyes, that hair bouncing
in the sun as he stepped off that
Mondrian school bus,
that smooth, honeyed tenor,
my adoration absolute, undivided, unbearable.

School was a distraction.
Teen magazines with names like
Tiger Beat sat on top of
open math books in class,
demanding to know how much I really loved David,
which I demonstrated with a D in math that term.

Solve for X?
Not while full page photos of that beautiful face
begged to be torn out of the magazine, taped to the wall
above my bed. The Partridge Family Album spun
over and over on the record player
I bought with berry-picking money,

my father rolling his eyes, sputtering how lyrics like
to be lovers when you're not in love

were nothing but crap, while I was certain they
were deep, profound, apocalyptic even,
since they had been formed by the lips
of a god.

In time, the pictures came down,
my father rolled his eyes at new albums,
and I solved for X well enough to earn a B.
Years later, news of David Cassidy's death brought
not sadness, but gratitude,
grateful he was on the fence with me

as I straddled little girl and teenager,
grateful for the exquisite agony of
Friday nights on the living room floor,
chin in hands, heart bursting, head throbbing,
rapt, tears coming hot and heavy,
childhood streaming down my face,

making way for the woman
yet to come.

VENERATION

I've always worshiped you.
The center of my universe,
the giver of life,

I needed you, could barely smile
when you weren't there.
I met you at the pool,

the beach, the park,
bared my body, my soul to you,
anointed myself with oil to attract you,

basked in the heat, the tingling,
the beads of sweat you drew
from my brow.

You made me blush.
We were happy for years
until, like an abusive spouse

who shows his true colors after marriage,
you went too far, left a mark.
They took a knife, cut it out,

called it cancer, blamed you.
Betrayed. I can no longer
leave the house without a coat

of armor to protect me from
you, the center of my universe,
the giver of light and life.

Helios, Ra, Sol Invictus,
Oh Sun, my Sun, faithless orb,
I thought you loved me, too.

WIDOW

You sit at home now
black in your anger
black in your grief
and you cry
and you remember
and you cry.

Tell me what it's like to be alone.
I don't know.
I lost only a father.
But you—
you lost a lover, a provider, a friend.
You lost everything.

So tell me how a memory can't warm a bed
or pay the bills
or bring you flowers.
Show me the old blue truck with his living
declared on the bumper:
Apples for Health.
Open the medicine chest and breathe in
the scent of Old Spice that still lingers.
Feed me his favorite Sunday dinner: roast pork and
your award-winning apple pie,
bake the bread from the recipe
that still sits on the spice shelf,
the last one he asked you to try.

Read to me from his beloved
Sherlock Holmes and Edgar Allan Poe–
Quoth the Raven "Nevermore."
Run your fingers over the epaulets on his
WWII uniform in the back of the closet and
tell me again how much you hate
carving your own turkey and being called
a single parent.

Widow mother
black in your anger
black in your grief
help me understand.

INTERLUDE

The half-life of love is forever.

~Junot Diaz

TREASURE CHESTS
For Lindsay

Two bookworms out for a stroll,
my niece and I,
on a mission to choose our next read.
She saw him first.

An old man with a long gray ponytail,
perpetual smile, a big colorful parrot attached
to his chest, clinging tight to his chest.
To his chest.

The bird was huge, red, green blue,
covering the man's entire torso
like Joseph's coat of many colors,
if that coat were alive,

its head stopping just under his chin,
feathers extending to his hips.
She and I exchanged glances, rolled our eyes.
A parrot attached to his chest

like a live brooch.
No harness or leash,
just claws digging into his shirt,
As I debated whether this was sweet or cruel—

to the parrot or to its perch—
he stopped in front of us, smile
firmly planted on his face.
We told him his bird was beautiful

and he, still smiling,
walked away.
Didn't think to ask if the bird had a name.
At the bookstore, we are mesmerized by

the likes of Faulkner and Lawrence,
Poe and Steinbeck, other authors unknown to us,
lost in the stacks, the smell of old books
sending us into a book lover's high.

Piles of books in hand,
chins raised, resting on the top
book, clinging to the treasures
attached to our chests like erudite jewels,

we see him.
Parrot Man, sitting on a dark dusty
couch in front of the stacks,
cooing softly to the

bird still clinging to his chest.
Outside, we lay our books
reverently in the car.
Lindsay turns, and on an impulse

I hug her, hold her
tight to my chest,
like the treasure she is to me.
like all treasures should be held.

ALEXANDRA'S LULLABY

Sweet little babe in your mother's arms
Safe and protected from the world's harms
Someday maybe you'll see
Just what you mean to me
But for now little babe,
Just sleep.

The world can be such a sad place
And when I look upon your sweet face
I want to dry your tears
For all the coming years
But for now little babe,
Just sleep.

Sleep my tiny child and dream
The peaceful dreams of youth.
For much too soon they turn into
The all too grown-up truth.

Oh the world is not such a bad place
For when I look upon your face
I see the promise of futures bright
Shining in your eyes tonight.
So close them tight
And sleep.

BUTTERFINGERS

For Laura, two years later

Another Saturday night
babysitting the three of you,
my sweet cousins—
LauraTracyandMichael—
like one word to me.

I didn't date
        or drink
                or party much in high school.
                    I preferred the three of you most weekends,
                        my personal holy trinity,
                    who would bring me the closest to a mother
                        that I would ever be.

Tonight we were baking cookies
and the flour
        or the sugar
                or the baking powder—
                    I really don't remember which—
                        slipped through my fingers
                    splattering the floor with white powder.

I rolled my eyes and muttered
I'm such a butterfingers.
You and your sister giggled and giggled
as little girls do—
Michael was too young to understand—
and from then on, I was Butterfingers.

Even 40 years later, when I pay you one last visit,
I bring a scarf for your chemo-bald head,
lotion for your chemo-parched skin,
and my eponymous candy bar,
for your chemo-shattered soul.

You are there
with your mother and your husband and your daughter
and your brother and your sister and your niece
and still more cousins
and I am overcome by the amount of love in that room.

It rises like the heat off a sweltering summer sidewalk,
swirling and swaddling, encircling and enveloping
everyone and everything there,
displacing the oxygen with its sweet, tender fury,
and I literally gasp for air.

Tracy giggles and giggles
as women do
and holds the candy close to you.
"Remember, Laura?"
she asks with all the wide-eyed exuberance
of that long-ago five-year-old.
"Remember?"

You nod, your brave face
swollen and bent in a smile that is
heartbreakingly
      unrelentingly
            tragically
                  perfect.
The perfect soccer mom
who once tried to explain off-sides to me
as we watched your little one play,
with a heart big enough to hold the world
and a brain that has betrayed you and is
      heartbreakingly
            tragically
                prematurely
                    calling the game.

I kiss you goodbye and later get the call
where, head in hands, I rage and
wonder honestly, which is worse?
Dying young?

Or living on and watching
as everything that makes the living bearable
            heartbreakingly
                    unrelentingly
                        tragically
                        slips through these damned butterfingers
                                    and is gone.

CHANGE OF VENUE

After being beaten blind so many times
the darkness feels like home.
The landmarks are familiar and
I make my way instinctively,
dodging obstacles, real and imaginary.
The imaginary ones are so much harder to dodge.
They tease and taunt, bullies that chase me back
and back into the darkness, where it is
safe.

But then you come along and flip the switch,
the brightness is jarring,
jarring. The light hurts my eyes, and I stumble.
You take my hand and lead me away,
away from the darkness that is
home.

Home. Moving out is moving on and
I'm not ready.
You point the way,
tell me I am safe now, but
I just don't believe.
I just don't belong.

But you take my cold hand and you warm it,
hold my breath in your gaze and you calm it,
put my heart in your care and you cradle it,
treating each beat as a gift
until slowly, slowly,
my eyes open wide to the light.

SONNET 1: LOVE SONG

So overwhelming is this joy you bring.
It gently strums my soul and taunts my lips
with words too sweet for human voice to sing.
I know the power in your fingertips,

the strength, the fire. I tremble at your touch.
You share my joy; I've let you taste my tears.
You taught me faith; I trust in you so much
I take you places inside me where I

have never welcomed visitors before.
You tell me that for us there is no end,
and no words in this world could please me more.
But that it's right, I can no more pretend,

for someone else, and though it makes me grim,
when reading this would think the words to him.

TO THE CHILD I NEVER HAD

I thought of you today.
You came to me as you always do,
without warning or context or provocation.
You're just there. Are you looking for something?
An explanation? An apology?

My dear little one, it's not that I didn't want to find you.
I really tried.
Your father and I dedicated our lives to
finding you for years.
We turned our bedroom into a chemistry lab
in hopes of discovering you
but to no avail.

We saw the specialists who promised to help us find you,
and we took their word
and their shots
and their pills
and their tests,
and they took our money
and our modesty
and all sense of normalcy
But they didn't help us find you.

We looked for you in their syringes
and their petri dishes
and their "alternative procedures"
but we still didn't find you.

And when one of them finally told us
we would likely never find you, even with their help,
I saw your father cry,
and I wondered why anyone would choose to specialize
in futility.

We looked to others to find you then,
but half-heartedly, I'll admit, because

it's a seller's market,
where irresponsible teenagers
who haven't the means or maturity to raise a child
are given the galling privilege of
judging and exploiting those who do.
If you were there, waiting, at the next agency,
or with the next lawyer, I'm sorry,
but we were numb.

We were raw.

We were done.

We turned your bedroom into an office
and chose to call off the search.

I carry snapshots of you in my mind—
opening Christmas presents with your cousins,
posing with your grandparents,
hair shining red in the sun,
graduating from college, standing so tall—
and I wonder if you are content with not being found,
if you know something we don't,
or if you wish we would have kept looking at all costs
like the woman in Iowa who with much intervention—
none of it divine—
produced her "miracle" litter of seven,
smug in her certainty that God would provide.
I can't believe you would want something like that.

So, little one, I'm afraid this is goodbye.
I have to let you go now. We're done.
Please forgive us, forgive me, we did the best we could.
And if the next time you come to me unbidden,
I do my best to push you away,
please, for both of us,
try to understand.

TAKE ONE

Take a page from my book.
Go ahead—take it.
Tear it out slowly and carefully.
Inch your way down gently so
you get the whole page and
it doesn't rip.
Take as many as you need,
for whatever you need,
for as long as you need.
But know that the wisdom
and the love and the truth
on those pages gave their all,
each word collapsing, exhausted, on the paper
like a dying soldier on the battlefield
who knows he fought the good fight.
So please, take a page from my book.
But remember,
tear slowly, tug gently,
little by little, inch by inch,
because like the phantom pain of a limb long gone,
that paper cut you'll get if you're too rough?

I'll feel it too.

SHE WALKS ON STARS

She walks on stars,
gliding effortlessly between them,
all angel hair and dancer's body,
arms extended, toes en pointe.

She asks no permission, assumes no license or
sufferance is required. She leaps, knowing
she will be received.

The stars twinkle and genuflect under her weight,
cradling her in warmth and light,
in all her guts, grace, and glory,
until each has imbued the other with its beauty.

When it is time for her to go,
there are no tears, no regrets,
only mutual gratitude and joy.
Arms extended, toes en pointe,

she glides serenely to the next, asking
neither forgiveness nor permission, knowing
she will be received.

I saw her once, long ago, this astral angel.
But she eludes me when I look
to the heavens now.

The stars are there, but no angel hair
flutters between them. They twinkle,
but do not bow beneath my probing eyes.

Perhaps she makes herself known only once
for that very reason—
so I know she is there,
so I know to keep looking,
to keep leaping,
to keep gliding,
all guts, grace, and glory,
we women who walk on stars.

BALLOONING OVER NAPA VALLEY

For Lorrie

We sat at your kitchen table and let you fuss over us
while we told you about our adventure.
You loved the idea of our balloon ride over Napa Valley.
You said it was the perfect birthday celebration
and that I had the perfect husband for arranging it.
You had so many questions—

> How fast did you go?
> How high did you go?
> Were you scared?
> Was it peaceful?

All the while your slender disfigured arthritic fingers
making us sandwiches from the
mackerel your husband caught
that morning,
all the while you making sure we were
fed and loved and made welcome,
all the while asking us

> how we felt
> what we thought
> what we wanted
> what we needed

all the while knowing your disease
was progressing and wanting,
I know now,
to breathe in and savor the scents and the sounds
and the sights and the feel and the flavors of us,
to absorb the very essence of us,
the essence of all those you loved,
and commit them one last time
deep into your soul.

We were there at the end.

As you breathed your last,
your husband gently took your hand,
and you released the warmth of that well-curated soul
into that cold room,
making sure we were all comfortable
one last time.
Now I had the questions—

   How fast did you go?
   How high did you go?
   Were you scared?
   Was it peaceful?

I cannot know, my dear cousin. I can only hope.

NO QUESTION

You wonder out loud if I will ever leave you.
You, who are everything I have ever been and ever will be,
everywhere I have ever gone or ever will go,
everything I have ever done or ever will do,

You ask this.

You ask this as if it is an option,
as if all these years were some sort of trial run,
or a can of beans with a Use By date that has passed,
or a warranty that has expired.

You ask this.

I see my reflection in your eyes—
all that is there is you and me and us and ours—
and in those eyes I see the proof that you are missing.
Look around, my love.

Your fingerprints are everywhere.

IT SHOULDN'T BE THIS HARD

Finding love is a crapshoot.
everyone knows that.
We start with our come-out roll,
laying bare who we are.
Few get lucky enough to win right there,
to avoid having to roll again.
Most of us shake the dice, blow on them,
invoke a higher power as we
roll again and again, praying for a match
before the dreaded number seven appears
and we lose.

Finding love is like a puzzle;
everyone knows that.
We walk through life holding our
puzzle piece in hand,
laying bare who we are,
trying it over and over again
on other pieces that look like
they should fit, appear to complete us.
Some find the perfect match,
nestle in comfortably,
but others settle for one
that doesn't quite click, force it.
Straining against the pressure,
the pieces burst,
destroying both in the process.

Finding love can be like a multiple-choice test,
everyone knows that.
We choose our answers carefully,
marking them boldly on another's
heart, dark pencil lead filling in the circles,
laying bare who we are,
knowing there is certainly a penalty
for guessing, desperately hoping

that even if they choose another answer,
they don't erase us completely.

It shouldn't be this hard.
If I could, I would make sure the dice
always landed on point and
seven never showed.

I'd see that puzzle pieces were made of
magnets and steel,
all the better to attract the right match,
the right fit, that resonant click.

I'd make sure every answer marked
boldly on a heart found its
match on a compatible heart,
that no one was ever erased.

I'd make it easier, make it faster,
make it work.
A little help, a little magic,
a new definition of
making love.

AQUARIUS, LIBRA, AND CANCER

The daily walk along the marina,
a brief escape from sheltering in place.
Heads covered in hats
to shield us from the sun,
faces covered in masks
to shield us from the plague,
but nothing to shield us from his news this morning:
It's cancer.

My husband walks ahead of me, looking into the water,
turns suddenly, pointing,
Look! A garibaldi!
his delight genuine, childlike, exuberant.
I remember one of his favorite stories
from his SCUBA days,
when the bright orange creatures
would surround him,
anxiously fish-kissing his diving mask,
while he carved up a succulent sea urchin for their dinner.
I smile at how he twists popular song lyrics
to insert the word *fish*
where it doesn't belong and
where it makes no sense,
singing them out at the top of his lungs,
just to see me laugh.

We look over the railing for his garibaldi.
My eyes bore into the water,
willing it to appear for him,
but it is gone.
He sighs and keeps walking.

He   is   my   world.
Is a single fish too much to ask?

ANOTHER DEAD RELATIVE POEM

I hate writing these.
They come at me like the undertow that
pulls the sand from my feet,
the foundation of family
wrenched away, leaving me
treading water yet again.

I apologize.
Each of you deserves your own poem.

My fierce and feisty aunt, equal parts
grit and graciousness, faith and family,
I should tell the story of your steel blue eyes
locked on me as you
guttered out your deathbed reminder to
take my medicine.

My bohemian cousin, you earned a celebration
of that wicked humor,
that tremendous sense of fun,
that mighty alto that I mistook
for a recording when you
begged Bill Bailey to please come home.

My father-in-law, I should laud your
immigrant tenacity,
engineering accomplishments,
the patents in your name,
remember your sweet smile,
thank you for your son.

But you all passed one after another
like a parade
with the drum major cloaked in black,
waving a scythe for a mace, instruments silent,
floats draped in hospital blankets
and rosary beads.

I stood in the bleachers,
bowed as you went by,
wondering when this march of grief
would end, looking to see if
anyone else I loved was coming
around that corner.

I'm sorry.
Each of you deserves your own poem.

I don't love you any less,
I just hate writing these.

PARFUM DE PARIS

I smelled Paris tonight.
At an outdoor summer concert,
in the midst of fried chicken,
pasta salad,
Tchaikovsky,
and the Hollywood Hills,
I smelled Paris.
That light, lovely floral that
welcomed me to the Hotel Ste. Germaine,
followed me past the flying buttresses of Notre Dame
down the River Seine,
and to the cafés of Montmartre.
Tonight I shamelessly followed the scent to its source
and asked her what she was wearing.
Sunflowers, she answered brightly.
But I know better.

It was Paris.

CRESCENDO

We have a world to conquer . . .one person at a time. . .starting with ourselves.

~Nikki Giovanni

DATELINE MOZAMBIQUE

"Why hasn't anyone come to their aid?"
asks the handsome newscaster

of no one in particular.
Floodwaters rising,

livestock drowning,
people missing,

and women giving birth in trees.
He does a suave segue into the local news:

silicone breast implants and
the rising cost of gasoline,

as if he just can't be bothered
with people

who didn't even have the foresight
to build an ark.

MIND TOGGLING

She sits on the bench at the bus stop on the corner,
clothes tattered, face streaked with dirt and teardust,
feet wrapped in layers of formerly white ribbons of bandages,
pathetic as makeshift shoes.

No one knows her story.
She screams obscenities at me and anyone who passes her,
we assume as punishment for our clean clothes, sturdy shoes,
pristine lives.

We ignore her as just another crazy woman
who doesn't know what she is saying,
who has no right to judge us or our
pristine lives.

She screams and curses, eyes wild and unfocused, and
I think maybe we're flattering ourselves.
Maybe it has nothing to do with any of us, but
someone who is not in the picture,

someone who may have earned this verbal assault,
but with whom she was mute then, by choice or by force,
someone who long ago abandoned her or beat her or left her numb.
We walk by and flip the switch,

and the memory, vivid now, enrages her,
the feeling returning to her battered body, not with
gentle tingling or pins and needles,
but with wild fury and indignation and pain that

in the absence of her long-ago tormenter,
she can only now release,
over and over again to anyone who passes her
sitting on the bench at the bus stop on the corner.

ENGLISH LESSON

*From our ancestors come our names, but from our virtues
come our honors. –Latin Proverb*

I got Karen'ed today, my friend's post read,
and I cringed.
My beautiful, talented, brilliant friend,
targeted just because she is Asian.

When did my name become a symbol of hate and intolerance
and why wasn't I notified?
There was no email, no memo, no petition—
not that I would have signed it—
but there should have been something.
I should have been consulted.

It took my parents two weeks
and a call from the County Board of Statistics
to come up with
Karen.
Blindsided because I wasn't the boy they'd wanted,
they tried on generations of family names before landing
on my two grandmothers':
Katherine Stella,
but those had already been recycled several times over,
and after the prod from the county
to please fill in my birth certificate
with something other than Baby Girl, they settled on

Karen (Norwegian for Katherine, meaning purity)
Estelle (from Stella, meaning star)

Karen Estelle. Purity Star. Hate and intolerance.
I don't see the connection.
I watch, puzzled and dismayed, as my solid, sturdy name
is taken in vain
to describe ignorant words or actions or people
that divide and demean and hurt.

Now I know how God feels.

OK, class, let's conjugate the verb "To Karen:"
I Karen; You Karen; He, she, or it Karens.
I do not Karen. I don't dare Karen.
No Karen would ever consciously Karen.

I got Karen'ed today, my friend's post said,
and a mutual friend reminded me that in Hebrew
a keren is a ray of light.
Pure light, pure warmth, pure illumination.

OK, class, let's try this again.
I got Karen'ed today, my friend's post says,
but this time, she doesn't hurt and I don't cringe.
Instead, we bask in the warmth of the
purest light that shines from us all.

AFTER THE FACT

Hostility and resentment
are all that's left, you say,
because months ago
I said it had to end.
Then, you said
you didn't need me,
I wasn't important,
it didn't matter.
But now you cry betrayal
and claim you've always cared.
I wish your foresight was more acute
because I never would have cut you
if I thought that you would bleed.

LAMENT FOR THE DAUGHTERS OF EVE

Apple, apple
evil thing
because of you we suffer.
Banishment from Paradise,
painful parturition.
From you we learned the naked truth.
Arrogant, seductive
you couldn't keep your
vast eternal wisdom
to yourself.
Good and evil,
right and wrong,
we didn't want to know!
You call yourself forbidden,
but just what do you forbid?
Apple, apple
evil thing,
You were only all too willing.

A MOTHER'S LOVE

She never forgot them.
Even after she gave them up, she watched from a distance as they grew and thrived
and reveled in their freedom and independence.

But she could never let go completely, and once she decided they belonged to her still,
she crept silently, stalking them, coming closer and closer
until they could smell her breath, feel the ache in her outstretched arms,
see the longing in her eyes,
the desire and determination etched on her chiseled face.

She watched as they played with their
cardboard guns, built forts,
pretended to be army men in the snow.
When she finally pounced, fierce and furious, she vowed to leave no child behind,
destroying their homes, their hospitals, their schools,
their souls.

Mother Russia does not bleed for her children,
she makes her children bleed for her.

Women in pom-pom hats plant sunflower seeds in the pockets of her soldiers,
cursing them,
while babas in babushkas and babies in buntings are carried from bombed buildings or
onto packed and stifling trains in hopes of escape.
Everyday citizens bear arms and bear witness to this cruel and inhuman mother
who would rain down bullets and bombs
against the innocent.

Her puppet sits in his gilded palace spewing lies
that flow like lava,
threatening to incinerate anyone who dares get in the way,
striking fear in the other children she once gave up that she would come for them next.
He sits in his golden chair, leering and lecherous,
opens their sacred book and
points a stubby finger at the fifth commandment—
Honor Thy Mother.

But the women in pom-pom hats, the babas in babushkas,
the plumbers and teachers and shopkeepers
who have traded in their toy guns
for real ones
and the boy playing the piano in an empty hotel lobby
as troops approach
turn one by one and show him their faces,
shaking their heads in unison.

No, they say. *Slava Ukraini!*

THE DOGS OF POMPEII

The stray dogs of Pompeii
slink quietly among ancient ruins
and modern tourists,
sidling up, begging for attention–
a touch or a treat–
from those too much in awe of the ancient
to notice the present.
They stretch out in long dry mosaic fountains,
look for the coolest spots to rest their heads,
the drone of preachy tour guides
washing over them like unholy water.

CAVE CANEM—
Beware of Dog—

a tired, tiled welcome mat at the entrance to
The House of the Tragic Poet,
unearthed from its lava tomb,
the faded mosaic warning of ancestors
apparently more ferocious
than these gentle souls.
Roman heavens held no angels,
so poets, tragic or otherwise,
relied on more earthly guardians.
With no need for their services
in this city—no longer home to poets,
lovers, merchants, or slaves—
the dogs of Pompeii now wander these ruins,
begging for a touch or a treat,
lazily crossing thresholds
engraved with warnings of the
ferocity of their ancestors,
oblivious to the irony.

MISOPHONIAC

I may ask you to please chew with your mouth closed.
I may ask you not to chomp your food like it's
the last meal you'll ever eat.
I may cringe when I hear you smacking your lips,
chicken leg in hand.
I may turn away when I see you wipe your mouth
on your sleeve, then let loose a deep
"Aaaahhh," like a balloon with a slow leak.
I may impatiently ask you to refrain from
clicking your teeth together while you chew,
because, really, if your teeth are landing on each other
and not on a mouthful of food, why are you even chewing?
I will likely leave the room after you clear your throat
the third time.

You get one.

I may lose my appetite if you slurp your soup,
clinking the spoon to the bowl after each gulp
in a rhythm reminiscent of the *Anvil Chorus*.

I will grimace at that squishing sound
as you smear a banana through your teeth
like you are frosting the roof of your mouth with it,
and I will excuse myself from the table
to go scream into a pillow if I hear you
suck your teeth like a Slurpee.

My name is Karen, and I am a misophoniac.
Google it.

I am working through this
one day at a time,
trying to follow my misophonia treatment plan,
but I keep coming back to the same question:

If you smack your lips
and click your teeth
and chew so I can see
every morsel of food in your mouth
and hear every chomp, snap, crunch, slurp,
crunch, and mastication,
and you generally eat like you were raised by wolves,
how am I the one with the problem?

POMP UNDER ANY CIRCUMSTANCE

He picked up the bowl
of power and caressed it,
smirking, smug, drunk on his own
delusions. He turned it over in his hands,

reveling in its construction and how easily
it suited him.. He paid his minions to
polish it, dust it off, wash it,
but in his eyes,

it was never dirty.
Any dust was someone else's fault,
someone else's fantasy,
fake news.

When it finally slipped, dripping with its
sick, slithering, shady ambitions,
through his greedy fingers and shattered,
he could have taken it as a sign

that dropping the lies, the deception,
these self-serving, entitled dreams,
was like shedding clothes that
no longer fit, no longer flattered,

that it was time to move on.
But like a gross perversion
of the ancient Japanese art of kintsugi,
he pieced it back together

with gold
and called it beautiful.

PRIVATE PITCH

Perfection.

Unattainable, impossible, unrealistic,
we are told. But in music, there is perfect pitch,
that ability to know with certainty
what note is being played or sung. Perfectly.
I envy those chosen few, those lucky ones, those savants,
as I, with my unblessed ear,
move to my own private pitch and
try to keep up.

But I've learned that what we see can blind us to
what we know.
We see perfect people and perfect houses and
perfect jobs and perfect lives,
but when it's all put under a microscope,
the roses dug up and the roots exposed,
we know that outside of that one musical gift,
perfect rarely is.

Perfect looks like the beautiful young couple,
gleaming teeth and pressed white clothes,
posing with their toddler who was lost to them
when someone mistook the accelerator for the brake.

Perfect looks like the house with the manicured lawn
in a tony neighborhood few can afford,
with pencil marks for children's heights along one wall
and police tape marking a crime scene on another,
the empty pill bottle and handwritten note marked
as evidence.

Perfect looks like the sweet Catholic schoolgirl
in a Mayberry small town
who is raped at gunpoint
walking home from a piano lesson.

Perfect rarely is.

Maybe even true perfect pitch
has a flaw we can't see,
wears a mask to hide its imperfection,
as we do, as I do to protect my
private fears, my private faults,
my private pitch.

SPEECHLESS

I could never say you hurt me because you said you never would and I could never say you didn't care because you said no one would ever care more and I could never say I didn't like being compared to your past lovers because you said it shouldn't bother me and I could never say your teasing was sometimes nothing short of cruel because you said I should know you didn't mean it and I didn't dare say you were unfaithful because you made it clear there'd be no strings and I could never say you beat that point to death because you had to make sure there were no misconceptions in our relationship and I could never say I was unhappy because you said you didn't like to see me that way so I finally said goodbye and you were speechless.

EMPTY

You cleaned me out again.
Like a voracious teenager standing at the refrigerator,
you gleefully ravage shelf after shelf,
chewing me up and spitting out the bones
like so much garbage.
But you shiver in the cold,
so I open my oven door
and offer up its warmth.

But the temperature is never quite right, and
I adjust and you reject
I adjust and you reject
until the cake can't possibly be anything
but a runny mess
and you skewer my incompetence.

In desperation
I throw open my cupboard doors and lay bare
what's left of me,
neatly arranged in efficient little rows
that you claim are not as neat as the neighbor's,
and with one dramatic sweep of your arm,
send crashing to the floor.
I am spent.
But because I am drained,
I am empty.
And because I am empty,
I am free, I am pure, I am lighter than air.
And as you rage
against this exquisite irony,

I rise.

I rise slowly and gently until I am above it all.
I rise until the mess below me hazes over
and I am out of your reach.
You rage and I rise.
You rage because I rise.
You rage and I rise,
and in that glorious moment
I know that from now on,
the kitchen is closed.

LIMITED

Scleroderma.
Lupus.
Hashimoto's Disease.
Raynaud's Syndrome.
All of the above.
Autoimmunity, the friendly fire.
My body fights itself
constantly, a battle
neither of us can win.
I'm lucky—they
say mine is mild,
aching joints, exhaustion, but
mostly
Raynaud's Syndrome.
Limited Scleroderma,
they call it. Sure,
let's call it limited.

Limited
       to cold hands,
       freezing hands,
       blue fingers,
       white fingers,
       numb fingers
       cold feet,
       freezing feet,
       blue toes,
       white toes,
       numb toes,
       even
in 70-degree weather.

Limited
       to a constant state of
       fight or flight,
       gratuitous spasms,
       blood rushing

everywhere but to my
hands and feet,
fingertip sores cracking through
because the blood
never got there,
pain enough
to bring me to my knees,
ulcerated, disfigured fingers
crossed that they heal before
too much tissue dies.
Tissue. Dies.
That's how I was diagnosed.
Too much tissue died and
my finger went black.
Gangrene.
Yeah, I went there.
Blue, white, red, black.
Unlimited color possibilities
for a limited disease.
Fingers. Die.
I gave up the guitar years ago.

Limited
to wearing gloves, finger cots,
carrying hand warmers,
enduring jokes,
explaining.
No, I'm not going skiing.
Yes, my hands are really cold.
No, these gloves are not a
fashion statement.
Yes, I CAN possibly be this cold.
Yes, I know I'm wasting water,
but it needs to be warm before
I can put my hands in it.
Blowing out candles,
wishing for the same thing for years:
just one day without pain.
Don't even wrap it—it's too hard to open with gloves.

Limited
>	to giving up smoothies
>	for breakfast because
>	I shiver for an hour
>	after drinking one
>	even
in 70-degree weather.

Limited
>	to dressing for Alaska
>	in LA. In June.
>	For flip flops, read Uggs,
>	for sundress, read sweater,
>	for linen, read fleece,
>	for shorts, read leggings.
>	Lined. In LA
in 70-degree weather.

Limited
>	to actually looking forward to
>	menopause, ready to welcome
>	a good hot flash, welcome
>	the warmth, welcome that
>	rush of heat, that freight train
>	my friends described,
>	the one that passed me by,
never stopping once.

Limited
>	to pretending I am normal and
>	trying to get through the arctic
>	cold grocery store without gloves,
>	hands so cold when I reach the
>	checkout line I can't feel them, can't
>	move them, asking the checker to
>	please take the credit card out of

my wallet for me, watching her
recoil
in 70-degree weather.

Limited
too, though,
to the sweet irony
that all this provided the exact moment
I fell in love with my husband,
when outside on a cool night,
he took my frigid hands,
put them around his waist,
wrapping them in his jacket
and the warmth of his body
until they thawed.

Unlimited.
That night these hands,
wrapped in warmth,
wrapped in safety,
wrapped in love,
these hands, my hands,
these flawed, disfigured,
icy, numb hands,
found home.

In any weather.

GETTY IMAGES

By the pool at the Villa,
shimmering blue and silver in the sun,
there is a model, blond hair thrown back,
pouty red lips, stick figure shrouded
in a flowing yellow floral caftan,
swirling, strutting, hips swaying,
sleeves falling long and wide at her sides.
Arms open, she seduces the photographer, enticing
him to stalk her on his feet, on his knees,

on his belly crawling, a starving dog begging
for any crumb she may throw, until,
with one haughty flip of fabric over a shoulder,
she is done.
On the other side of the pool
an older woman poses for an unseen camera,
loud, shrill, wild gray hair, skinny legs painted
in watercolor leggings,
arm around her teenage daughter,

shrieking *Don't be ridiculous* as her
daughter, dark hair covering her face,
black sweater pulled around
ample breasts and hips,
arms crossed to hold it tight,
pleads for a photo just from the neck up,
just their faces by the pool.
Please Mom, just faces, no bodies.
I know this girl.

I was this girl,
long dark hair covering my
"but you have such a pretty" face,
always delivered as if it were
wasted on the likes of me,
Rubenesque body, arms crossed in front,
holding tight the sweater, holding tight the shame,
joking about breaking the camera
before someone else did.

I want to tell this girl to flaunt her own
floral caftan, open her arms wide,
let go the sweater, let go the shame,
throw her hair back, seduce the world
with her worth, because sometimes
with mothers shrieking, models
swirling, cameras clicking, girls like her—
girls like us—

can forget it's there.

YOSEMITE'S CHILDREN

The day dawns beautiful, clear, cold.
Wearing our weight in jackets and socks,
we set out early. The trail extends ahead,
revealing the steps of those before us.
The deer, the bobcat, and perhaps the hare—
all have left their mark, as we leave ours,
moving to the satisfying crunch
of snow under our feet.

I sit and raise my head to the sun
amid trees dripping tears of melting snow
that fall like gentle rain all around me.
So many trees stand charred,
scarred, scorched—remnants
of the last wildfire, omens
of more to come. The innkeeper this morning
said he doesn't like summer anymore.
It's too hot. Too parched. Too dry.

We are too hot. We can't see the forest
for the trees, but we can't seem to see that
without the trees, there would be no forest.
Without the forest there would be devastation,
drastic climate change, soil erosion,
loss of home for the deer, the bobcat, the hare,
leaving a much bigger imprint than those
sweet tracks in the snow behind us.

The river below runs smoothly, swiftly,
leading us back to the road, back to the town,
back to the inn, back to the ignorance of bliss.
I wonder out loud why there are no pinecones.
Then we see them: row after row of
new growth, tiny pine trees in their receiving blankets
of snow, the elders hovering over them with pride.

The big trees watch as their offspring
sprout from their seed and reach for the sky,
granting us one more generation,
one more circle of life,
a little more time,
opening their arms to us, exposing their
might and their vulnerability, their beauty
and their wisdom, trusting that
eventually we'll get it right.

CODA

Light be the earth upon you,

lightly rest.

~Euripides

CHASING THE SUN

A Saturday at nearly dusk, rooftop deck,
fruity cocktails in hand,
sitting spread out in wide, coral-colored Adirondack chairs,
the good life.
Catalina Island is shrouded in clouds in the distance,
the Four Preps coo from our
carefully curated summer mix
about longing to be there,
twenty-six miles across the sea,
even though we know it's only twenty-two.
The Beach Boys lust after surfer girls,
The Drifters sing about how our cares will go away
now that we're up on the roof
Sly Stone, Mungo Jerry, Jimmy Buffett go on about
hot fun, fine weather, that one particular harbor
and Pablo Cruise invites us to find our place in the sun,
an invitation we graciously accept.

The sun slips a bit,
and I look out toward the island
to see a cruise ship heading south,
a container ship heading north,
a sailboat heading nowhere in particular.
A hawk circles the neighbor's yard,
gliding and hovering, diving and dipping
between house and clouds
before drifting lightly onto a telephone pole
to plan his next move.
He slowly lifts his wings, takes off, flies directly
into the sun,
straight to it, gliding and hovering,
Icarus evolved,
feathers unencumbered by wax or warning or
doubt. I can't look.
I sip my cocktail, think
maybe my feathers need to be ruffled a bit,
groomed for flight,
shed their waxy excuses for looking
no higher than the roof
for heaven.

SONNET 2: AUTUMN SONG

I watch my autumn sunset slowly sink,
and now my winter's knocking at the door.
The welcome mat is out, but still I think
I'd like to go back to my spring once more

to see the girl I was through older eyes
and let her know the world is bigger than
the place her broken heart is forced to lie.
I think a kindness it would be to plan

a visit to that heart now that I've learned
that life is bumpy, rough, yet still is sweet
and time arranges all things in their turn,
that love will someday ask to take a seat

within her soul and she will let it in.
Brave girl, that day you let our life begin.

PARTS UNKNOWN

I

Once a decade you managed it,
Lady Lazarus rising from the dead
or almost dead.
Your confessions rolled off the page,
all agony and genius,
razor blades and prodigy,
torture and brilliance,
no apology or appeals to bless you,
for you had sinned. Sin was
irrelevant.
Once a decade you managed it,
but once in one decade
you couldn't.
You were through.

Sylvia Plath
1932–1963.

2

Rock star of the culinary world,
rough, rugged, crude,
unapologetic, coming out
of one addiction to feed another,
finding a place in the professional kitchen
of misfits.
Restless, always restless,
no lasting refuge,
searching the world for
that one eye-popping, heart-pounding, mind-blowing,
culinary high to keep the torments
at bay, those confidential
kitchen demons that burned in your gut,
fiery and red-hot,
until they burned too bright,
and you followed them to
parts unknown.

Anthony Bourdain
1936–2018.

3

Comedic genius,
always on, always shining,
always going for the next laugh,
seamlessly switching
characters, accents, personas,
as easily as switching hats.
Easier.
But *O Captain! My Captain!*
your influence was strongest
when we, the poets and musicians,
the artists and dreamers,
heard you speak to us,
tell us that engineering and
medicine and science are
noble ways to make a living,
but poetry, beauty, romance, love—
these are what we stay alive for.
O Captain! My Captain! I wish
they were enough for you.

Robin Williams
1951–2014.

4

Clipped lines, terse verse
old man of the sea,
Nobel prize winner, ambulance driver in the
war—the other war, not the one
in your brain. Hard drinker,
killed lions for sport,
but kept housecats with six toes.
Womanizer, woman hater,
trouble chaser or trouble magnet—
not clear. Bullfighter,
truth-teller, genius, egoist, hedonist,
victim of too many mental patient
brain blasts. Quiet the bells,
the bells of doubt, of torment, of brilliance,
the bells of exhaustion.
Quiet the bells that tolled
for you,
that toll for us all.

Ernest Hemmingway
1899–1961.

BIRD STRIKE

I hear the thud and I know.
The bird, a little finch,
lies motionless on the chair
outside my window.

Looking up, I catch
the predator's eye
of a Cooper's hawk
perched on the balcony's edge,

long, squared-off feathers descending from
a sturdy dappled body, talons
clinging to the stucco as if
he'd done this before.

We stand and stare,
daring the other to flinch,
daring the other to make a move
toward the listless creature on the chair.

The hawk blinks first,
nods in concession,
stretches its powerful wings,
and takes off.

I sigh, grab a shoebox, plan a funeral.
But the little finch stands, stunned,
shaking, tests its wings, lifts up
and flits away in the opposite direction.

Smiling, I think
how wonderful it is
that sometimes all it takes to save a life
is simply showing up.

ASH WEDNESDAY

Remember, if you will, the carnival and the
Man with the sad dirty face
That haunts you still.
You with your mask and feathers
Are strangely attracted to him, like the
Dust on a treasured photograph
And he knows better than
To blow it away, since he is wearing the same
Dust that forever seeks out the neglected.
You turn away, but you know you
Will search for him when you
Return, for like the dust,
You   will   return.

JESUS IN JUNE

He won't come in the fall,
apples crisping, Eden molting.

He won't show in winter
on the heels of his birthday.

He won't arrive in spring,
tulips and hatchlings bursting with life.

I expect to see Jesus in June.
The sun takes the month off here,

the sky a constant gray haze,
ripe for a warm burst of light,

a glorious descent,
a promise kept.

However we salt our Jesus,
with Rome, or Luther, or fire and brimstone,

or if our diet is Jesus-free,
we dream of comeuppance,

consequences for
evil, hate, deceit,

sins committed against us,
against the world.

Judgment delivered, justice
served cold, gray, June.

We have faith, or not, but we hope.
We follow the golden rule,

turn the other cheek, display the
swaddled manger baby every Christmas,

search the sky in June,
just in case.

MIDNIGHT SONATA

I. Exposition

I do not sleep.
I hear it is a lovely place, sleep—
a place of rest, of bliss,
a place where dreams are made.
But I do not visit often.
My eyes close, I try the door,
but it does not open easily.
I see the welcome mat under my feet,
but my key doesn't always fit,
no matter how many times I jiggle the lock,
and I've learned not to force it.
Sometimes a poem will come, or
lovely memories of the day,
but often the company I keep
in the dark is a rough crowd
I try to avoid in daylight—
doubt, grief, fear, anger, regret.

II. Development

And then I hear him—
the owl that lives in a nest nearby,
but visits the cypress tree
outside the bedroom window,
the tree the Romans called
the Mourning Tree,
the one that points toward heaven.
A great horned owl, they say.
I've never seen him, only
heard his solemn, low-pitched
hooting song,
plaintive and ominous,
sometimes quiet and barely audible,
often loud and deliberate.
I know why he is there.
The yard is a menagerie,
a cafeteria of prey for him—

skunks, rabbits, cats,
mice, squirrels, rats.
If his hunt has been successful,
I haven't heard it.
I understand nature taking its course,
the circle of life,
but I prefer to think he sings
for me.

III. Recapitulation
He does not sleep.
His song is sincere,
but I know it is not for me.
I say a silent prayer that his
hunt is successful, that
I don't hear it if it is.
His cry grows fainter, I
pull the blankets in tighter.
My eyes flutter, then close.
Still he sings, low and slow,
this rhythmic grace before dinner,
this accidental lullaby.
I try the key in the door once again.
It turns. For a few hours, maybe,
I will sleep.

LAST RITES

Don't bury me with my resentments
unresolved, living hidden underground,
waiting for the company of my bones to keep them warm.

Don't bury me laid out in my prettiest dress, painted in
ghoulish lipstick and rouge, hands crossed primly beneath
my sagging breasts, clutching rosary beads I rarely touched in life.

Don't bury me in fertile earth better suited to growing
food for the living; sacred ground that should be sprouting
corn and carrots, not corpses.

Don't bury me in a huge steel box meant to preserve me, so I take up more space
dead than I did alive. Let me return to dust
to complete the circle of life; the one job the dead are tasked to do.

Don't bury me in a huge oak box, lined in tufted satin, top flung open,
all filing by, gawking, proclaiming how good I look dead.
Pay me your respects now.

Don't bury me with a sad-eyed stone angel, hands raised to the heavens, guarding
my grave, as if the others without such servants are less worthy.
Angels should guard the living.

Don't bury me. Burn me,
and offer a few of the ashes of my days as communion with the wind.
Let it carry me off to places unknown—one last road trip.

Let the rest remain in something small and simple,
marked only with my name and dates.
I leave it to you now to remember or imagine

the story of what transpired between those dates,
since it is too rich, too complex to fit
on a small square plaque on a small brass box.

ECLIPSE

The lovers sit, hands enfolded tightly,
neither wanting to let go for fear of
ripping open the gaping hole of their lives.

In the distance a choir is singing
a requiem for the moon,
the *Dies Irae* dark and low,
warning of justice and punishment and
unparalleled wrath, growing ever more ominous
and foreboding, shrouding the moon in black
like a nun who hides behind her habit.
Dies irae, dies illa.
This day, this day of wrath.

The lovers cower, terrified, afraid to look up,
until faint light returns through their tight shut eyes,
eyes that they raise together now
to see not death or doom,
but the moon, pure and whole,
still shining in its heaven,
their innocence spared.

The choir grows fainter,
fortissimo fades to *piano*,
throaty baritone bends to sweet soprano.

Alleluia,
Alleluia,
Amen.

NOTES

Limited, page 58

> For more information on scleroderma and Raynaud's Syndrome, contact the National Scleroderma Foundation at scleroderma.org.
> For more information on lupus and other autoimmune diseases, contact the Lupus Foundation of America at lupus.org.

Photo Credits:

Cover

> iStock, Getty Images

Pg. xii *Prelude*

> iStock, Getty Images

Pg. 2 *Summer Fruit*

> Orchard – Karen Basiulis
> Author with her father circa 1968, author's collection.

Pg. 16 *Interlude*

> iStock, Getty Images

Pg. 40 *Crescendo*

> iStock, Getty Images

Pg. 50 *The Dogs of Pompeii*

> (Top) :iStock, Getty Images
> (Bottom) Karen Basiulis

Pg. 65 *Yosemite's Children*

> Karen Basiulis

Pg. 68 *Coda*

> iStock, Getty Images

Pg. 71 *Chasing the Sun*

> iStock, Getty Images

ACKNOWLEDGMENTS

Many thanks to the editors and publishers who first published some of the poems in this book and to the contest judges who awarded honors.

- *Prolific Peninsula: Palos Verdes Library District Anthology 2019,* "Ballooning Over Napa Valley."
- Writing the Waves: Palos Verdes Library District Anthology 2020, "Mind Toggling."
- *Poetry Project of the Arts Council of Torrance* (video), https://www.youtube.com/watch?v=FnRzVSqGA58 "Butterfingers", "Empty", "English Lesson", "Mind Toggling", "Widow", September, 2020.
- *Lummox 9 2020,* "Dateline Mozambique", "Ash Wednesday,"
- *Spectrum, Spring 2022,* "To the Child I Never Had."
- *"Quantum Entanglement, Poetry Apocalypse Anthology", 2023, "Last Rites" (titled as "Requiem Realistica").*
- *Arts Council of Torrance Poetry Competition, 2nd place, 2018,* "Full Crate, 50 Cents."
- *Arts Council of Torrance Poetry Competition, 1st place 2019,* "Empty."

SPECIAL THANKS

I owe a huge debt of gratitude to the following people:

To my friends **Laurie Delman**, **Lisa Nygren**, and **Vicki Fleisig**, who reviewed the poems, who lifted me up when my confidence was waning, who always told me it would be worth it.

To **Linda Neal** of the Redondo Beach Library Poetry Workshop and **Linda Singer** of Poetry Apocalypse, who were the first to welcome me back to the world of poetry after I retired and decided it was time, and who reviewed this manuscript with their perfect poetic eyes and experienced candor.

To **Tommy Domino**, my instructor at Community Literature Initiative, who offered tremendous encouragement and gave me the nickname "Word Nerd," a badge I wear proudly.

To **Lisbeth Coiman**, who insisted I apply to CLI and made sure I followed through.

And to my husband, **Al Basiulis**, who warms my hands and my heart, who always knew this book was in me, who never let me give up. You are everything.

ABOUT THE AUTHOR

Karen Butier Basiulis was born and raised a farmer's daughter in Watsonville, California. She has been writing prose and poetry since childhood, coming back to poetry seriously after retiring from an extensive career in project and contracts management, mostly in the aerospace industry. Her poetry has appeared in several literary magazines and her essays have appeared in professional journals and newspapers. She has been a singer most of her life, from her start at St. Patrick's Church in Watsonville, to Carnegie Hall and Europe, holding a Bachelor of Music degree from California State University, Long Beach, and a Master of Science in Systems Management from the University of Southern California. She lives in Los Angeles with her husband of over 30 years and two semi-feral cats.